Finally Noticing

Photos and Poetry
Prompted by a Pandemic

Anne Garrett Spry

Finally Noticing: Photos and Poetry Prompted by a Pandemic
By Anne Garrett Spry
Page Design by Cheri Battrick

Copyright 2022
All rights reserved

ISBN 979-8-9858031-2-9

Personal Chapters LLC
Wakarusa, KS and Independence, MO

Contents

Morning Pandemic Prayers	1
Enough Food and Toilet Paper	3
Settling into a Pandemic	4
Prepare the Way	6
Morning Contrasts	9
Clematis and Stone	10
Double Rainbow	13
Goodbye Sweet (sort of) Summer	14
Fall Prophecy	16
Covid Thanksgiving	19
My Sunrise Evolution	21
Song of Hope	22
Humble Blossoms	24
Snow Lillies	27
Upslope Fog	28
Hopeful Skies	31
A Gift of the Present	32
Noticing the Dawn	35
Interpreting Covid Sunrises	36
Storm Sunday	39
Fall Sandwich	40
Whispers of Glory	43
Fourth Dimension Sunrise	44
Please Notice Me	47
Tuesday Ta Dah!	48
Leading Edge	49
Untitled (God's Brushstrokes)	50
Untitled (Lewis Caroll)	51
Uvalde Meditation	53
Welcome, July 2022	54

Kenyon and the Rain	56
Goodbye Sweet Summer	59
Pointing to Heaven	61
The Sum of All Our Skies	62
The New Covid Church	64
Finally Noticing	66
Postscript Positivity	68
Photo and Graphic Credits	70
About the Author	73

Dedicated to my grandchildren–Cooper, Charlotte and Camden. They will inherit all the manifestations and challenges of the Post-Covid world.

Prologue

I don't consider myself a poet, or even a photographer.

I hated studying poetry in school (and in a twist of irony, even wrote a poem about that recently). My experience and university degrees were in journalism. Photographing news and sports was something that just came with the territory of editing and publishing a weekly newspaper for 27 years. I got by with aging Nikon equipment and detested working in the darkroom so much that the advent of digital photography became a reason to celebrate.

Enter the pandemic of 2020. I was officially retired by then but newly dedicated to helping others record and publish their personal history, In the initial days of the pandemic, my powers of observation intensified, and found an outlet in poetry and photography. Beginning in March of 2020, I also journaled, blogged, vlogged, and learned new technology as I struggled–like most of the rest of the world–to make sense of a new way of being. Like many of you, I tried to stay connected to family and friends through social media. As the lockdowns and social distancing morphed into a new lifestyle focused on home and hearth, I got quiet.

Suddenly, I became grateful for this worldwide pause and really noticed the beauty of God's creation. While trying to discern reasons to encourage myself and others, I discovered new hope and a conviction that God had not abandoned the world. My early morning and evening walks became a prayer of gratitude for the beauty I now saw everywhere around me. I'd come in the house with a fresh set of photos, pick the one that spoke to me the most, post it on Facebook and begin to type on the screen… until the words formed themselves into poetry.

The feedback from friends filled me with encouragement and even more gratitude. The message I tried to convey then and want to transmit now in this little book is that God still loves us, no matter what goes in the world at large. The beauty of His creation is a gentle nudge to love him in return; and to never lose hope.

Anne Garrett Spry

Morning Pandemic Prayers

"And the people stayed home. And read books, and listened, and rested, and exercised, and made art, and played games, and learned new ways of being, and were still." **(From a book by Kitty O'Meara, who has been called the Poet of the Pandemic)**

My addition to this poem would be
"And the people sang. They sang
John Michael Talbott's 'Come Back to Me'.

My morning prayer is similar to O'Meara's,
But not nearly as eloquent.
I look at my suddenly free calendar,
Ask to find blessings in pandemic-speak,
In social-distancing and self-quarantine.

I beg for the ability to prioritize things
Most beneficial for personal growth, and
To aid loved ones from solitary confinement.

Is this killer virus leading us all to repentance?
Will we now focus on the people and the thoughts
Most crucial for our survival as a culture?

Please tell me, Lord, that toilet paper hoarding
Is not how we learn to behave in a crisis.

Shelves at Walmart, March 2020

Enough Food and Toilet Paper

I finally venture out on a pandemic afternoon,
Finding empty aisles disturbing.
No dry cat food, no cereal.
No eggs or fresh meat.
Only a few canned goods.
Social distancing is hardly possible
in a Walmart on a Pandemic Friday.
An employee says the eggs, hamburger,
and toilet paper shelves were full
when they opened at 7, but empty by 8.
Is this a new Black Friday, with shoppers
waiting every day for doors to open?
Is this a new bottom rung, added In 2020,
to things Maslow said we really need?

Settling into a Pandemic

Smoke from prairie burnoff camouflages the sun.
A mama bluebird settles down for the night while
Humans hunker down in their own houses to watch
Mindless network episodes of true crime stories,
Avoiding the more painful realities of a
World gone mad with fear of an invisible enemy

March 31, 2020

Prepare the Way

Fog blankets still morning waters
As the Paschal super moon recedes,
Making way for another beginning that
Shines on this less-traveled highway.
The world quietly prepares for
A Resurrection.

April 8, 2020

April 27, 2020

Morning Contrasts

Lighter, budding-out leaves against evergreen hue.
Dandelion fluff contrasts with high cloud fleece.
Storm-cloud dark is lit beneath by lighter-sky blue.
Oaks cast long shadows on rain-soaked ground.
Wind sighs counter mockingbird calls,
and an endless to-do list butts heads with
morning's soul-quenching contemplation.

Clematis and Stone

An inanimate creature
Appears to nestle
Against a bosom of bloom
While we who are animated
Turn hearts formerly cold
Back to a Savior.
We're all little children,
His forever to hold.

May 17, 2020

June 10, 2020

Double Rainbow

Unusual morning rainbow in the western sky,
Intensifying first on the northern end
Before turning into a double arch in the south.
Is the clear demarcation between dark and
Light skies a message for this era?
Can we anticipate peace and untroubled days
To be ushered in on winds of change?

Goodbye Sweet (sort of) Summer

The red summer welcome, once splashy,
Fades into weeds and spent blossoms.
The primary 2020 visitors here have been
Hummingbirds and my sighs of discontent.
Tiny birds have no clue the human who fills their feeder
Mourns the lack of children's laughter and
The swift passing of her favorite season.
Even the sunrise looks faded this year.
A late summer sunrise only slowly dries the dew
Yet is warm enough to chase low-lying fog
Before its full beauty is captured and preserved
In the pasture across the road.
The wannabe windmill,
normally a whirling dervish
in relentless Kansas winds,
Lies silent with dew. Waiting.
Even the spent butterfly plant below
Waits inside a sea change while
Late-blooming clover absorbs the paradigm shift,
Seeding itself mindlessly, meekly.
We humans cling fearfully to
The odd side of reality
With faith our only anchor.

August 22, 2020

Fall Prophecy

Candy corn sun
So similar to the one that
Hung there in March.
Australian wildfires then,
California and Oregon's today.
As the spring sun signaled the advent of a pandemic.
May the fall sun foretell an end to all the endemic
Viruses and smoke and political polemics.

September 18, 2020

Covid Thanksgiving

It was just the two of us yesterday.
So strange, so quiet. No noise but our chewing.
Neither of us had seconds.

I took a photo of him; he took one of me.
We needed to mark the odd occasion,
Record it for posterity, noting the austerity.

No lively conversation, no real celebration.
But later we rejoiced in phone calls, texts,
A grandson's quick visit to drop off ham loaves, and

Recall the relative who always made them.
We savored memories in the meat and it
Reminded us of the purpose and meaning of this day.

Let us pray for the return of exuberance next year,
Of chaos even, and yes, over-indulgence too.
And may we all be thankful for this gentle pause,
In the year that most of us chose caution and isolation.

My Sunrise Evolution

Until coming back to my birthplace in Kansas
I hadn't recognized the state's bragging rights
For spacious skies, stunning sunrises and
Epic, sweeping sunsets.
And now I also must brag.
It is, after all, a sacred trust.

Songs of Hope

Music will go on, no matter what.
Even if we have to distance ourselves
And sing behind two masks.
God breathed the notes into our souls.
They must come up and out of us
In worship and in hope.

February 21, 2021

Humble Blossoms

How does it do it?
A simple little apple tree.
Quiet, unassuming, timid.
It doesn't advertise its beauty.
It doesn't call out, "look at me."
Yet I walked up close and heard
My camera. Or was it my breath,
Inhaling sharply in recognition
Of the contrasts embedded in
the humility of a tree.

April 13, 2021

April 18, 2021

Snow Lilies

Do they shudder
From their safe perch inside
While outside a rare scene unfolds.
Or do they just gaze in wonder
Glad they can now hide
Safe in store-bought disguise
At least until blossoms drop off
Summer falls and
They go in the trash.

Upslope Fog

Funny thing, this morning fog.
Like rose-tinted glasses
Or a camera obscura
It hides the finer details
Of things we usually miss
On our rushed way.
But we did stop,
We breathed in.
We noticed today.

May 10, 2021

June 4, 2021

Hopeful Skies

Could there be anything more hopeful
A better, more perfect way to start a day
Than to spy a sky full of fair-weather friends
Once we shift our focus from feet to heaven

A Gift of the Present

For the first time all summer
We sat outside on the swing
Watching the storm slide
Down out of Nebraska
Felt the breeze on our faces and
Listened to a tree frog.
We went in at dark, reluctant
Yet relaxed and refreshed
From finally living in the present.

June 23, 2021

July 22, 2021

Noticing the Dawn

They're never the same
These sunrises and sunsets.
They leave distinct fingerprints
On the horizons of our days
Sometimes feeble, sometimes transcendent
More often glorious and reminiscent
Of the Creator of the skies.
We cannot recall growing older,
Yet we have done so under many
Unnoticed dawns and dusks.

Interpreting Covid Sunrises

How many sunrises and sunsets,
Rapturously captured and bottled with a click...
What compendium of news broadcasts
With charts and graphs showing ebbs and tides...
How many friends' and relatives' funerals,
How much self-isolation and meditation...
Will it take to fathom the whys and hows
Now that we're weary of the whats and whens.

August 9, 2021

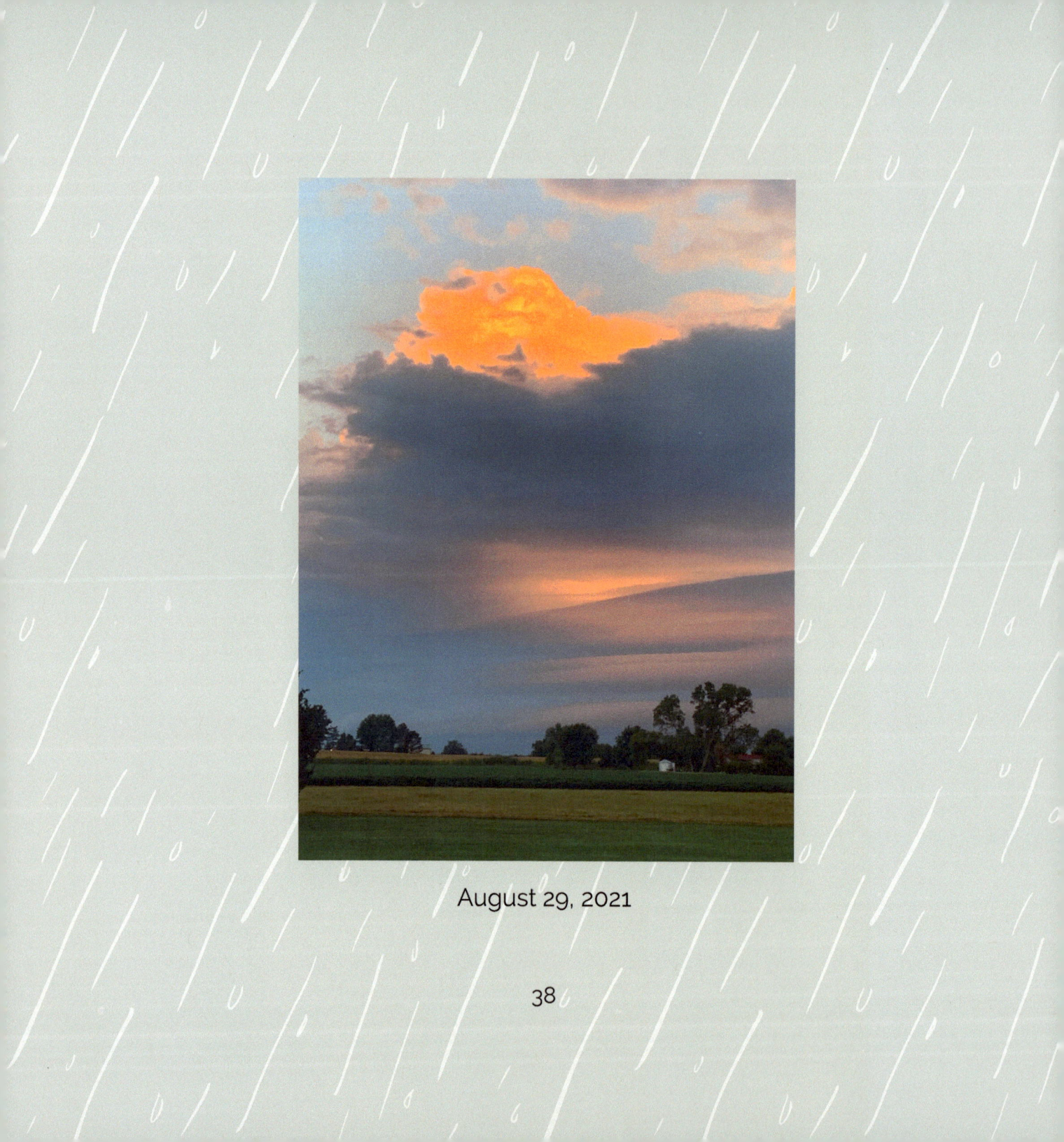

August 29, 2021

Storm Sunday

I captured the front progression on a morning walk.
It changed perceptibly, second by millisecond,
while my family near the Gulf has no time
to stand and gawk. They get ready to evacuate.
Their storm approaches from the sea.
The Midwest version develops north and west.
Words failing, I stand in Sunday worship.

Fall Sandwich

Patterned Western textures of sky-blue coral
Oppose Eastern dissipated hues,
Illuminating landscape layers
That begin with domesticated emerald,
Graduate up to empty, round-baled terrain
Before showing just-now-turning-gold beans,
Shadowed by the brittle brown stalks of autumn.
This is Earth's sandwich–
a movable feast for the soul.

Octoer 5, 2021

November 11, 2021

Whispers of Glory

I sat screen-staring in my upstairs office
when a chance glance out the window
revealed clouds set in vivid contrast
against a cerulean sky.
I saw images made by wind, moisture,
a changing barometer and
constantly evolving season.

Sometimes God whispers.
Today He shouted Glory Halleluiah.

Fourth Dimension Sunrise

A Kansas sunrise always entices great shots,
this morning's especially so.

Bare trees, leaves ripped off in brutal winds,
no longer inspire except in silhouette
against full daylight skies.

I now prefer surprise sunrises or magic dusk
toward which to aim my iPhone 13, with its
special time-lapse night default.

I relax, inhale, and let IOS 15 do its thing.
It led me home, into a zone of wistful awe,
Revealing promises of a fourth dimension,
And glimpses of our inevitable road home.

November 27, 2021

January 4, 2022

Please Notice Me

As I sat journaling on a crisp winter morning
Something teased my eye corners, whispering
Look up. Get your head out of your belly button.

Notice me. Stop worrying. Stop fretting
about new infections, friends' breakthrough
Cases or your own inevitable one.

All is going according to plan.
The sun still rises, beauty and love abound.
Notice it. Live it.
Love it. Share it.

I live and work in, through and despite all things.
I aim for your ultimate good and eventual reward.

Tuesday Ta Da!
Wolf Moon descending.
Glorious morning rising.

January 18, 2022

February 1, 2022

Leading Edge

Here it comes,
Fair warning
This morning
Of forces we can't control.
But being the humans we are,
We just have to do something.
We jump in our cars
Skitter down store aisles and tempt fate,
Pretending bread and milk will pre-empt
The Impending Snowpocalypse.

February 10, 2022

They're called medium altitude cirrus clouds.
I prefer to call them God's brushstrokes.

April 21, 2022

"Oh frabjous day, calloh, callay"
It's a Lewis Carroll kind of day.

May 27, 2022

Uvalde Meditation

We close our eyes,
Slow our breathing,
Picture them in light,
Calling on our loved ones,
Even pets on the Rainbow Bridge,
To usher them into pure love,
Urge them on to a better realm
Far away from violence and
A bullied youngster's hate.
We see them in white rays
Reflecting back to earth
Surrounding parents, friends
And all the rest of us with hope.

Welcome, July 2022

The first hibiscus bloom greeted me
with a big front porch hello, and
a patriotic splash of welcome.
Every day for the past week
I've looked at the buds impatiently
wondering if there was any substance
hidden there and if this season would be
a repeat of unmet expectations.
But God always provides His own timeline.
Why did I ever doubt?

July 2, 2022

Catnapping to Kenyon and the Rain

Shoes kicked off, legs on the couch
covered in quilted sunflowers, I inhale comfort
from my bookshelves. Bracketed by pillows,

I listen to softness pitter and slide down the window.
The little dog stretches out long on the carpet below,
both of us settling into cataracts and arthritis.

She teaches me how to just be,
while Poet Jane Kenyon, gone since '95,
gives us words to soothe and shutter our eyes.

Goodbye Dear Summer

Fog intensifies and curls
around trees with gray kitten tails.
But August arrives tomorrow
on hummingbird wings
bringing a sense of loss and
worry. Have I made the best of
linear time? Was I in the now
enough instead of in my head,
Isolated, out of touch, selfish?
Then it dawns–the self-reminder
that annual melancholy always
descends when the locusts sing.

Pointing to Heaven

Glimpses of heaven in eastern skies.
What a privilege to be an earthbound
Witness and notice the magic in
Raindrops on petals pointing to God.

The Sum of All Our Skies

Monday sunrise. Add in Tuesday
morning skies and there is
always something different
to delight and surprise our eyes.

The New Covid Church

Close down, the authorities said, in April of 2020.
We reopened a few months later, only to close again.
We prayed, we learned to stream, and we held worship
with a preacher, pianist, and a techie,
while the pews sat empty.

No funerals, no weddings, no ham and bean dinner.
Few made donations, tithes fell off. Yes, we lost members
but kept streaming, kept praying,
kept trying to avoid copyright issues
from broadcasting hymns on YouTube.

When the numbers finally dropped (infection, that is),
We tiptoed back in, first with masks, then without.
We gladly greeted friends and neighbors
and felt so grateful that a pandemic
could not destroy the faith or the place
that God and determined humans built up in 1878.

Finally Noticing

Now that we've been through it
we know what a pandemic looks like,
sounds like, feels like, tastes like, grieves like.

Now that we know we can co-opt life,
avoid the masses, huddle inside,
fear the worst, work from home,

order online, and live in virtual reality,
some of us choose to recuse ourselves
from such trials and tribulations.

Some of us drew the lucky straw,
missed the Covid lottery, got the arm jabs,
tossed aside fears, went for walks,
prayed, meditated, expressed gratitude.

We finally noticed, finally lived,
loved and laughed again.
We refused to put the C-word in all caps,

rejected living as co-voidants and now we choose
life with a Capital L, recognize the need
for repentance, know our only choice
ever—in all of history—was and will forever be
LOVE.

Postscript Positivity

Thunder rumbles, rain pelts windows dim-lit by a
November cold front pushing through.
A great day to read a book, eat tomato soup
with grilled cheese, nap sitting up.

It's as good a day as any to be housebound by Covid,
the monster I have feared for two years.

It's a good day to lose taste and smell, with a new
bitterness coating the tongue, while shoulder aches,
coughing and dripping nose bring unaccustomed misery.

While I endure a virus that has changed the world,
will I be different on the other side?

Am I paying the price of self-indulgence
for leaving the safety of rural Kansas to enjoy
unmasked hugs and smiles with formerly virtual friends,
to bond over stories, conference sessions, and local cuisine,
only to go home and text sneeze and cough emojis?

If I had stayed well, would my focus
have remained diluted, or reverted to
the old arrogance, the old nonchalance?

I admit I knew the world was changed, fragile,
yet heretofore ignored it. Now that I have
met the enemy, found him less than fierce,
will I grow into a new optimism?

The fall shower brings relief to a parched land;
so too this viral bogeyman, now that it's found me.
I have survived...am surviving...this November storm,
and hope the world will be washed clean in due time.

Photo and Graphic Credits

All cover photos and all interior photos by Anne Garrett Spry.

Background graphics throughout the book are from the following:

- p. 1   leaves-303538_1280 by Clker-Free-Vector-Images from Pixabay.
- p. 2-3   shopping-4059182_1280 by Mohamed Hasan from Pixabay. shopping-3225130_1280 by Burhan Khawaja from Pixabay. Path Dashes by Handriwork from CanvaPro.
- p. 4-5   birds by RoundiconsPro from CanvaPro.
- p. 6-7   fog background by AdobeStock_135262071
- p. 8-9   White Watercolor cloud by Lianna's Creations from Lheay Creatives from CanvaPro.
- p. 10-11   floral vines outline by Aidenopoly for CanvaPro.
- p. 12-13   Pastel Rainbow Illustration by ozricsCartoons from CanvaPro.
- p. 14-15   Dandelion Time Background by des111gn from CanvaPro.
- p. 16-17   Corn Line Icon by Puckung from CanvaPro.
- p. 18-19   Illustration of Maple Leaves by Open Clipart-Vectors from Pixabay. Maple leaf by vectortradition from CanvaPro. Hand Drawn Oak Leaf by Helen Reveur from CanvaPro.
- p. 20-21   Floral by Gordon Johnson from Pixabay.
- p. 22-23   Clef Music Note by GDJ from Pixabay through CanvaPro.
- p. 24-25   floral-297687_1280 Clker-Free-Vector-Images from Pixabay.
- p. 26-27   Snowflake icon by Mositron from CanvaPro. Snowflake Christmas Singe by sunnyrabbit from CanvaPro. Snowflake by Mositron from CanvaPro. Snowflake Christmas single element by sunnyrabbit from CanvaPro. Snowflake Icon by Canva. Layouts from CanvaPro.
- p. 28-29   White Smoke Effect Design by Amelia Yan from Yan's Images through CanvaPro.
- p. 30-31   Sun rays by Bakuden Creative from CanvaPro.
- p. 32-33   Curl by Harmonia Green from CanvaPro. Swirl Line Art Illustration by Ahsanjayacorp from CanvaPro. Calligraphic border by Harmonia Green from CanvaPro. Swirl by Harmonia Green from CanvaPro.
- p. 34-35   Illustration of Sunset by stediaco from Pixabay.
- p. 36-37   Simplified Mughal Natural by Sketchify India from CanvaPro.
- p. 38-39   Raindrops Outline Illustration from Curlyscribbler on CanvaPro.

p. 40-41   Illustration of Farm White Wooden Fence by Yulia Drozdova from CanvaPro.

p. 42-43   Central light rays by R-Designs Criativos from CanvaPro.

p. 44-45   Road Vector Illustration by zmicierkavabata from CanvaPro.

p. 46-47   Leafless tree Illustration by OpenClipart-Vectors from Pixabay through CanvaPro.

p. 48-49   Tree Branch2 by Aleksander from CanvaPro.

p. 50-51   Cirrus Clouds Illustration by Silvetstrip from CanvaPro.

p. 52-53   Angel by Aurielaki from CanvaPro. Vector Image by Open Clipart-Vectors from Pixabay.

p. 54-55   Hawaiian Lei Tropical Flower by bokasana vector from CanvaPro.

p. 56-57   Sunflower Frames by HB Share from CanvaPro.

p. 58-59   Designer Curl by Sweetgrace from CanvaPro.

p. 60-61   Transparent water drops isolated by from ellengold's images on CanvaPro.

p. 62-63   White blue sky gradient background vector image by asamack92's images from CanvaPro. Round light ray by alvin dolicto siluet strip from CanvaPro. Cumulus cloud illustration by AlieniZed from Pixabay through CanvPro. Purple Gradient Hand Paint by Mystikal Forestfrom CanvaPro.

p.64-65   Light by raansya from Sya's Design through CanvaPro.

About the Author

Anne Spry is a retired newspaper publisher who started a new career as a book publisher in 2014. She never imagined writing poetry, but a friend urged her to audit a poetry class at Washburn University in Topeka. Now she lets the poetry muse loose occasionally, whenever she needs a break from other writing and publishing projects.

Anne and business partner Cheri Battrick recently teamed up to publish a journal and guidebook for a masterclass they are currently piloting called ***Writing to Heal: Journaling with Jesus to Find Perspective and Hope.*** She has written and published a memoir, a true crime book and published dozens of titles for clients.

Spry is married and lives in Wakarusa, KS with husband Wayne, three dogs and a cat. She may be contacted by email, AuthorAnneSpry@gmail.com. Connect with her on Facebook at https://www.facebook.com/annegarrettspry.

www.ingramcontent.com/pod-product-compliance
Lightning Source LLC
Chambersburg PA
CBHW040722060526
44119CB00083B/299